Gift of Initiation:
How Bhai Manj Changed Sant Mat

Adapted from a story told by Sant Ram Singh Ji on
January 2, 2016 & January 9, 2017

Illustrated by Carlos Brito

GO JOLLY
BOOKS

Gift of Initiation:
How Bhai Manj Changed Sant Mat

Gift of Initiation is a story originally told in Satsangs by Sant Ram Singh Ji on January 2, 2016 & January 9, 2017 during Meditation Retreat Programs at RadhaSwami Ashram, Channasandra Village, Karnataka, India.

Special thanks to those who reviewed & critiqued the story:
some sevadars

Translated by Ashok Shinkar
Transcribed by Ali Czernin, Geoff Halstead, & Harvey Rosenberg

Carlos Brito continues to create illustrations that bring joy to our hearts and smiles to our faces. His style of illustrating adds beauty to our world and helps others forget their hardships, even if just for a moment. Once again, his magical illustrations complement the words of our story and make this an outstanding book for both young and old. Thank you, dear Carlos.

ISBN-13: 978-1-942937-22-7

(c) 2017 All Rights Reserved

Published by
Go Jolly Books
www.gojollybooks.com
P.O. Box 2203, Port Angeles, WA 98362 USA

FIRST EDITION, GO JOLLY BOOKS, First Printing 2017
10 9 8 7 6 5 4 3 2 1 Printed in the U.S.A.

Gift of Initiation:
How Bhai Manj Changed Sant Mat

Adapted from a story told by Sant Ram Singh Ji on
January 2, 2016 & January 9, 2017

INTRODUCTION

Gift of Initiation: How Bhai Manj Changed Sant Mat shows the difficult tests Bhai Manj had to overcome before and after initiation. Because of Bhai Manj, our lives have been made much easier before and after receiving initiation (even if it doesn't always seem that way to us).

Gift of Initiation is a beautiful story demonstrating the great love, faith, and devotion Bhai Manj had for his Master. Even when Bhai Manj experienced great personal and family loss, he never lost faith in his Master and continued to obey Him. Bhai Manj is a wonderful example for all of us.

In January, 2014, at RadhaSwami Ashram, Channasandra Village, Karnataka, India, Sant Ram Singh Ji gave me permission to take stories He told in Satsang and publish them as books.

He told me to make sure the books were for children. This meant I could change His words directed to adults to words more suitable for children. With His Limitless Grace, reviewers of the first ten books have told us children like the books.

Once again, Carlos Brito has given us vibrant, alive, strikingly-colorful illustrations to accompany the words. His joyful use of color make up the whimsical characters and beautiful scenery. Like our other story books, Gift of Initiation: How Bhai Manj Changed Sant Mat, will impact children's and adult's understanding of our most beautiful Path. We hope you enjoy it.

Radhaswami,
Harvey Rosenberg

Dedication

There are not sufficient words to express our gratitude to Sant Ram Singh Ji for His Limitless Grace in making this book so beautiful that both adults and children will appreciate and love it. Without His Grace, there would be no book.

After a wealthy and influential farmer, Bhai Manj, listened to Satsangs of Guru Arjan Dev, he felt transformed and requested initiation.

In those days, initiation wasn't as easy to receive as it is today. Masters gave Their disciples difficult tests before and after initiation.

Guru Arjan Dev Ji noticed that on Bhai Manj's land, there was a tomb of a Sheikh where all the villagers offered their prayers.

Guru Arjan Dev Ji told Bhai Manj, "Remove that tomb from your farm, level that land, and then come for initiation."

That night, Bhai Manj gathered some farmhands, cleared away the tomb, and flattened the land, because he was keen to get initiated.

When Guru Arjan Dev Ji saw within that Bhai Manj had followed His instructions, He initiated Bhai Manj. At the same time, He started testing his faith, love and devotion.

In the morning, when the villagers saw that the tomb was gone, they were unhappy. They felt that Bhai Manj had done something wrong and started criticizing him.

Bhai Manj didn't pay heed to what they were saying, but villagers stopped farmhands from coming to work for him.

They wanted Bhai Manj to repent for destroying the tomb, but Bhai Manj refused. He just obeyed his Master, Who continued to test him.

Some of Bhai Manj's cattle and horses died, a few family members died and others deserted him. Also, he was unable to work his farm, because he had no farmhands.

Seeing this, villagers taunted Bhai Manj, "This misfortune is because you destroyed the tomb. Re-create that tomb, and then you will escape these hardships."

But Bhai Manj refused. He maintained his devotion to his Master, even though he no longer had any income.

This forced him to sell land parcels to meet his living expenses. After three years, he owned no land. He, his wife and their twelve-year-old daughter were destitute.

The family decided to leave, because no one would give Bhai Manj a job. They tied two bundles, one of clothes, one with utensils, and moved to a place where there was water and farmland. There, Bhai Manj built a small hut and got a job as a laborer.

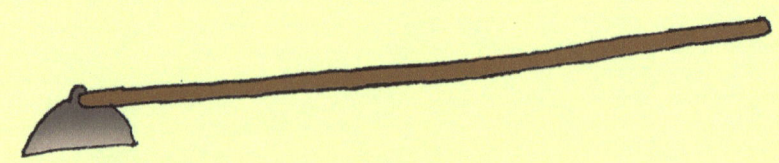

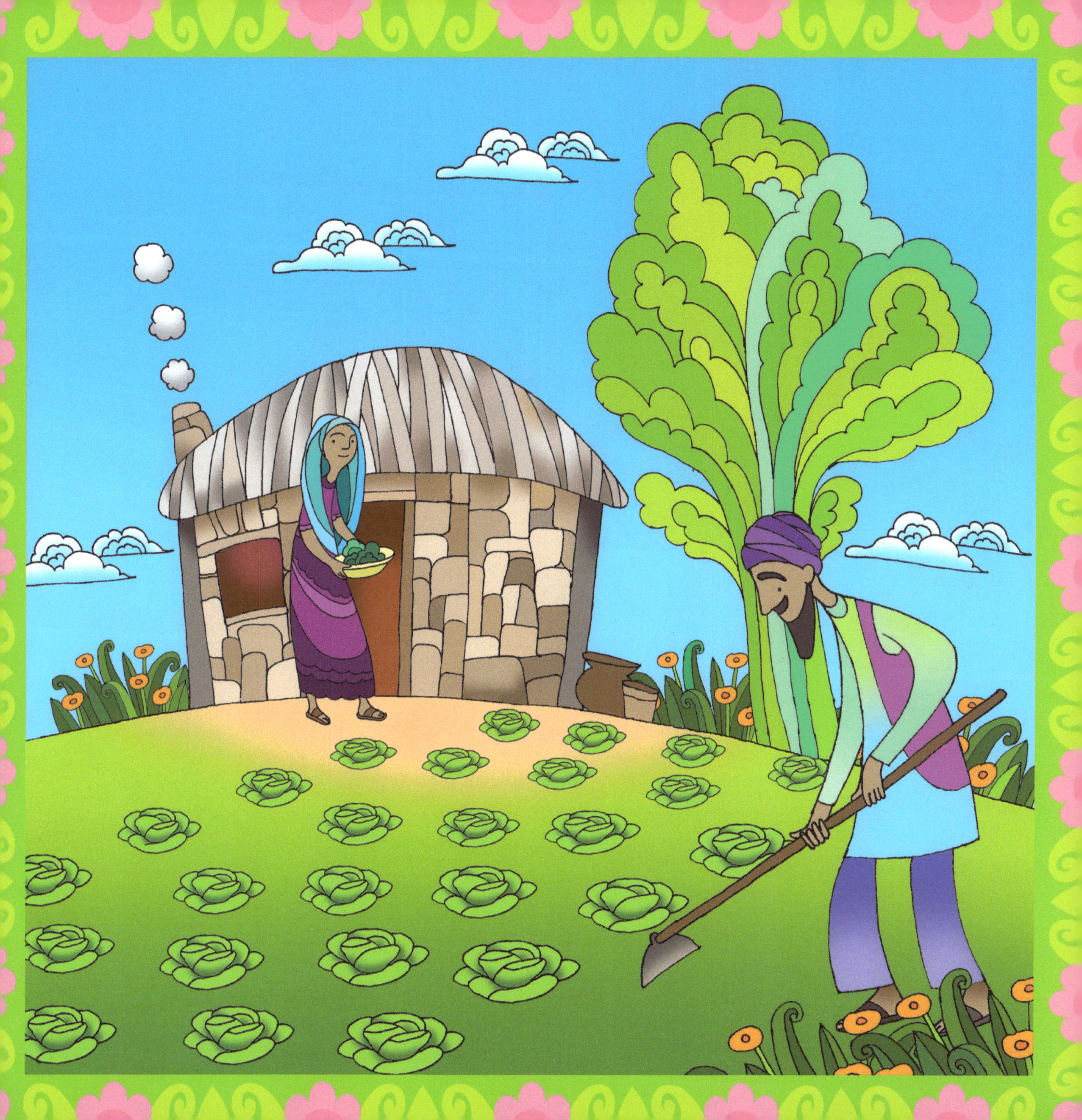

After six-months, Guru Arjan Dev Ji wrote Bhai Manj a letter. He told the sevadar, "Hand-deliver this letter to Bhai Manj, and ask him for twenty rupees before you give it to him."

The sevadar brought the letter to Bhai Manj, who was very pleased that His Master had remembered him. When Bhai Manj asked for the letter, the sevadar said, "Give me twenty rupees first, and then I will give it to you."

Bhai Manj didn't have the money, so he asked his wife, "What can we do to get twenty rupees?"

His wife found some silverware and gold jewelry she had saved. Bhai Manj exchanged it with a jeweler for exactly twenty rupees.

He gave the twenty rupees to the sevadar, and then read the letter, which said, "How are you? I hope this finds you in good health. I'm also fine here. Good wishes to you."

Bhai Manj was thrilled with the letter and happy that his Master had thought about him. Sometimes he touched the letter to his chest, sometimes to his heart, sometimes to his eyes, all of which made him joyous.

Another six months passed. Arjan Dev Ji wrote a second letter and sent it again with a sevadar to Bhai Manj.

When Bhai Manj asked for the letter, he said, "You have to pay me thirty rupees first."

Bhai Manj didn't know what to do, but remembered there was a wealthy farmer nearby. The farmer had asked if his son could marry the eldest daughter of Bhai Manj.
Although Bhai Manj had refused then, he went to the farmer now and asked if he had another son that his youngest daughter could marry in exchange for thirty rupees.

That farmer was a wise man and aware of Bhai Manj's condition. The farmer felt that Bhai Manj's daughter must also be suffering these hardships. Why not do what Bhai Manj is suggesting and take her into our family? Then, his daughter will also be happy and well taken care of.

He accepted Bhai Manj's offer, married the young girl to his son, and gave Bhai Manj thirty rupees.

When Bhai Manj opened the letter, he read, "In whatever state you are right now, come to the ashram."

He immediately told his wife. They packed their frugal belongings and walked for about a day and a half.

When they reached the ashram, the first thing they did was to line up to receive the Darshan of Guru Arjan Dev Ji. Bhai Manj bowed to the Guru, but Guru Arjan Dev Ji ignored him and looked the other way. He pretended not to notice Bhai Manj, so Bhai Manj took the Blessings and walked away.

And whenever they went for Darshan, the Master always looked the other way.

Six months passed like this. One day when Bhai Manj's wife came for Darshan, the Master spoke to the person in line in front of her. He asked him, "Has Bhai Manj come to the ashram?"

His wife overheard the sevadar's reply, "Yes, he came six months ago and is doing seva."

The Master said, "What is he doing?"

The sevadar said, "They are doing seva in the ashram, and they eat here also. They live here."

"If he's doing seva and he's eating, then what value is he adding to the ashram? Both are equal," the Master replied.

Bhai Manj's wife told Bhai Manj about this incident. He agreed, "Yes, Gurudev is correct. We are eating here and doing seva, but we are adding nothing to the ashram. Let's stop eating here."

Bhai Manj advised his wife, "Clean the utensils twice a day, but don't eat in the langar. Early in the morning, I'll cut firewood and make two bundles, one as seva and the other to sell. With the money I get, I'll buy food for us. That way we both will do our seva without taking anything from the ashram."

About a year passed. Daily, Bhai Manj brought firewood from the forest to the ashram and a second bundle to the market, where he sold it and bought food for himself and his wife.

Once while doing this, a fierce thunderstorm struck with strong winds that caused dust to blow in all directions. Bhai Manj was carrying both bundles of wood when the wind pushed him backwards, and he accidently fell into a well with about four feet of water in it.

It was nine o'clock in the morning when this happened. Guru Arjan Dev Ji was giving Satsang. He stopped and immediately ran towards the forest and the well, about two kilometers away. All the people in Satsang wondered why the Master had left so quickly, and they raced after Him.

His sevadars also followed. Guru Arjun Dev Ji told one of them to bring a ladder and rope. He instructed them, "Go into that forest until you reach a well, where Bhai Manj has fallen. Get him out of that well."

Guru Arjan Dev Ji purposely stopped a short distance before the well to hear what the sevadars would say when the Guru wasn't there.

When they reached the well, they asked Bhai Manj to take hold of the rope and climb out. He said, "No, first take this firewood, which is for the ashram."
They said, "What are you talking about?"
Bhai Manj replied, "This wood belongs to my Guru. I have to give that first."
One sevadar said, "What 'Guru', 'Guru', are you talking about? Because of your 'Guru', 'Guru', you've lost all your wealth, your farm, you've lost your family, all your possessions, and now you're stuck in this well."

This upset Bhai Manj, who said, "No, no, don't talk like this about my Guru. Say whatever you want about me, but don't speak badly about the Guru."

Then, they said, "Okay, we'll ease the ladder down into the well."

Bhai Manj tied the rope around the wood and it was pulled up. Then, Bhai Manj climbed out.

That's when Guru Arjan Dev Ji ran to the well and embraced Bhai Manj. He blessed Bhai Manj and said, "Whoever you give Naam to will go straight to Sach Khand."

And then Guru Arjan Dev took Bhai Manj's soul back to Sach Khand.

Guru Arjan Dev next said, "I'm very happy and pleased with your seva. Ask whatever you want and I will give it to you. If you want, I will take Kal out of the three planes and give you these three planes to rule."

Bhai Manj replied, "No, no, no, I don't want these three planes. If I have a Sat Purush like You, then I don't need any other thing. What am I going to do with all of that?"

Guru Arjan Dev Ji repeated, "I'm very happy with your seva. Ask for something."

Then Bhai Manj said, "There are going to be very difficult days in Kalyug as we go forward. My request is that these kinds of tests not be given to the disciples. It will be very hard for disciples to meet such tests in the future."

Guru Arjun Dev Ji agreed. When a Saint makes any decision like this, then All the Saints follow that and All respect that. And that is why now disciples do not have to pass such difficult tests.

Bhai Manj took all that pain and underwent all those difficulties, but what he asked was for the benefit of everybody.